POEMS FOR MY FBI AGENT

C000265453

Charlotte Geater lives in Waltha........ ... . and writer, and volunteers at a community library. Her poetry has appeared in *Queen Mob's Tea House*, *The White Review*, *Clinic* and *The Best British Poetry 2013*. She won The White Review Poet's Prize in 2018.

Poems for My FBI Agent

Published by Bad Betty Press in 2020
www.badbettypress.com

Cover design by Amy Acre

Printed and bound in the United Kingdom

A CIP record of this book is available from the British Library.

ISBN: 978-1-913268-06-0

Supported using public funding by
ARTS COUNCIL ENGLAND

LOTTERY FUNDED

poems for
my fbi
agent |

PRESS

poems for
my FBI agent

for Tom

Contents

poem for my FBI agent

my agent is pretty cool; he arrives late
& would skive off early
if they let him.
no suit, but he wears big black sunglasses.
he gets ten minutes every morning
for coffee, & in the afternoon he uses
his break for tea
& to check the week's weather.
my FBI agent feels the strain
—mostly it falls on his eyes—
when i take selfies he's curdling
towards a cluster headache.
my agent can't afford to live anywhere big
—a shared apartment in a mid-sized city
but he does ok.
half-full milk carton in the fridge,
the kitchen tap leaks at the base.
in his open-plan office, desks stretch
out too far. too far back.
he's lost count of his colleagues,
of the messages i send.
a pile of disposable coffee cups,
disposed.
there, on the other side of the glass.
knocking for me.

my FBI agent doesn't like to read

but guess who is the other key member
of my radical book club!
i read a lot of ebooks because i am always thinking
of him
                    and his lack of access to an academic library
marxist monetary theory
kate millett's sexual politics
william morris biographies

am i teaching him to like
reading? to bend himself around
each line
i like to read
through his eyes
after i have read using mine or sometimes
when the tea brews right & my brain fires off
at speed
                    it ricochets back and folds in &
i can see each page twice at once
a small crease in the middle
two screens

one of us is prone on the ground
one of us is running
one of us is looping back around
one of us is lying
down

sympathy for my FBI agent

my FBI agent is underpaid & would like to sell
my soul/data/camera roll
      but i never do anything interesting.
my agent has never made
      love on the clock, is nearsighted
and shaky with a gun.
he didn't do so well at his yearly review
& it's hard to know what to say.

how about here? how about lower?

sometimes he misses
important events
in my life, when he's taking too long
over his lunch, or trying to get in those hours
on the gun range

he's sick of all the carly rae
and the increasingly improbable covers
of 'girls just want to have fun'. my agent
got to agent school too late
for classes on deciphering handwriting

and reading what is meant by
the shapes our hands make

my FBI agent grows familiar

we're not friends. he knows me better

than that. there is nothing forgiving
in his gaze, and nothing that i
can forgive.

do i make it into your dreams?
i dream of battery farms
& rabid dogs. my agent is there

and despite his dark glasses and heavy vest
we both know the dogs' teeth
will hurt

him no less than me. *you are not safe,*
my voice says. he shakes beside me.

my FBI agent is a mathematical problem

and not just a philosophical one. if i ask who watches
the agent
who watches me, it sounds
insincere; but let's get down to it
in our underwear & most vulnerable body parts
who's at the other end of the line?
who does he text when he's lonely?
who gets to see
his underwear, and stricken texts?

if i type a poem instead of writing it out first
it feels closer to god, by which i mean
closer to you, watching me
and if i am not a problem, are you there?
do you only appear when i call for you? my agent
are you only
looking out
when i look back
matter changes when it's hit
am i a problem for you yet?
the lake turned to ice improbably fast;
and the custard became a rock inside your mouth.

my FBI agent talks me through my facebook ad settings

mass media / narrative / sunday / victory / year / grammatical tense
/ romanticism / everything (band) / genre / spectacle / organism
/ emotion / women's rights / walter benjamin / maria sharapova /
phil spector / carly rae jepsen / hybrid (biology) / grammar / verb /
nike (mythology) / petticoat / pocket / fandom / aesthetics / sound
/ gender / tennis / family / sabotage / books / instant messaging /
institution //

i say: is this how you see me?

birthday in october / close friends of men with a birthday in 7-30
days / close friends of ex-pats / commuters / gmail users //

i want to know about data in poetry when it's bad data & i want
to know about how you see me in these systems when they're bad,
i don't mean morally, i mean shitty, incomplete, i mean you know
too much and it's all worthless except. except for the ways in which
it works for you. i struggle to get out of bed & some days all i keep
down is tea with milk in. you say: interested in victory, pop music by
murderers, and grammatical tense.

i don't know whose birthday is in 7-30 days and you're making me
feel like a bad friend.

a lot of things are true / a lot of things inside me are not so

i want to know what data looks like from the inside. my agent, do they pay you enough for laser eye surgery. cleansing light. clearer now. scratching out the imperfections. how easily can you access the drive that i am writing this onto. i am scratching each word in a place where neither you nor i can lose it. in the short term. in the drive. in this tepid bath of many years, but not centuries. maybe software's fragility will save us. maybe i want everything i write to be saved.

the earliest prehistoric art is ochre. i type ochre as achre, over and over, as if creating a new word and somewhere i wonder if it's in this error that you see me. if in the strange keystrokes you register, you know me better than before i wrote this poem to you.

an archive of keystrokes / is that what you see

and i wonder what red means to data. i wonder about the loss, about the losses that you know. the feeling of files and data, your lost memory, the lack of something else. a broken backspace key. only being able to go forward. never. back back back

my FBI agent watches me take off my shirt

for once i have a bra underneath
only a sports bra; it's too small

        so i pull at the elastic hem
and think: is he there

no light running / no alarm / no whirr of the fan

deleted photos; a soft click
        lets me know my phone
                isn't on silent, the roll
of the camera from this shot
            to a shot in the half-dark
wondering why i stripped down to watch
              bogart in the maltese falcon
PrtScr + Ctrl only who cares about
          you've got access to more
              of me
                 than right now
                 thinking
                 at night
                 exposed

i undress to movies; take my dressing gown off
first at odd hours because i need to put on clothes
to feel alive / like, did you know there's a world
out there

i have taken photos with this webcam
grainy / unflattering / smeared

in the half-dark from watching a movie
on my laptop screen even though there's a television
right here because if it's not a cinema

why not commit to the degradation

my FBI agent is envious

of my trip to the theatre
i turned my phone off before the show started

nobody wants to be an accessory
to bootlegging a musical!

if you wouldn't steal a cd
                    it's your responsibility
to make sure
                    the experience
of living in that room
                    crying songs jumping
that living in tune
                            and out of key
it's your responsibility to be sure
                                that nothing
                    is stolen
from you

my FBI agent appears to me in a pub in leytonstone

and until then it was a good night
love-struck by railings
thin neon letters, the first light of spring

walking back and forth down
wet kisses in the air / but not raining
the railings scratched smooth
to my hand, sleeves dragging

who fears the sky

sediment in each glass i down
thick skins, i always liked
how you taste.

it's not far enough from the past
who passed me in the hallway,
pint glass shook up, sediment
left streaked / cloud trails

dead sand churned up
to make new land or just concrete

it's not past / so fuck the portrait behind the bar
the queen is still alive and i refuse
to drink / sedition, i said

which sounds like a beer name
which sounds like

the man who turned to me at the bar
and said be careful, there are lots of royalists here

or "there's lots of wireless here—"

i'm listening / press a glass to the wall

plum grains at the bottom of the glass.
everything tonight felt harsh
on my throat and i didn't drink whisky
even but the man at the bar did

and who's afraid of a painting
and who fears the sky
and who sticks around way too late past closing
and whose finger
sticks into my glass for the grains

mist; the rain to come
smog; the sediment

my old painted boots. the man turned away
and forgot what he said.
and my hands are dirty with cat fur
and dirty plum skin

rubbing at my own skin
where it's overdue
flake / shed

a date pit hidden in my pocket
and struck with love for spring & this new street
new to me

trails of water in the
who fears sky, out here.

i tell my FBI agent an old communist joke

except i replace the word "comrade" when i talk
to him and then there are times i wonder

what it means

that i made a person where a system lives

did you hear that, comrade lieutenant?

let me know if the lighting in here
hurts your eyes

let me know if you're finding it difficult to see
or if anything about my current set up
or tone of voice
makes it hard for you to interpret the feeling
of any particular scene
in front of you

like the mint plant in the kitchen

i am desperately trying to keep alive

my FBI agent tells me about the bureau's diversity policy

the rest of my character
is soft flesh, my beating

the moment your knife nicks

a good way to get me to trust you: ask to see
my hardest truest or softest parts
& see them, apart

& say that they will not hurt me anymore

a good way to get me to trust you is: these few short years
which show on your face and mine.

i mean such a big moon outside
i mean such a light i had not seen before
only inside, only hands, & my friends

it is not often that i raise my voice to say:
you have never been my friend

excruciating specificity & wrongness & the seductive stare
of someone who really knows you
trips / a single nerve

your breath turns me transparent

i wear a mask & reclaim some mystery
nobody knows who murdered me;

you can see my legs
beneath these stockings.

form is a form is /
drop down to me on your knees

and say: i am older now

and my heart is a soft hiccup
and you can tell who i am from my voice
and some mornings would have murdered me for it
and some days would favour

me with a pink token, a rash of flowers
and say:

my lady, i see you for the thing you are
and it is for you i fight

i see that you are old now, dear night

unarmour the sky / sheathe

what you promised once burns on your skin.

what i say in anguish
what i wear in love
what i cried on lately:

this is not your data / and yet the shape of my letters
are what you may burn me for

in turn. turn on my arm a while

before you change your mind
and turn to the beat & bass once more.

my FBI agent is selling my data

but he keeps copies for himself
printed out and stored in box upon box upon box upon
he strokes the smooth reams
so much more than a body
of evidence; me in my pink cap
from fifteen different angles

bodies frozen everywhere, like dance diagrams
time collapses outwards, sets free
too much *stuff*. how did everything get in there.
how did my body exist

and how will you bury me?
how long will it take to burn? another way in which
time does not make sense of accumulation
& destruction is against all time
against the depth
building

i destruct myself within

no clock can tell you when
out on deck
all seas ahead, and no way of knowing
where i will end up
or which of my bodies is moving;
which will be left behind

my FBI agent takes a holiday

he watches foreign birds through binoculars
this time he's the visitor

mud doesn't stick to his trousers
no sand in his sandwiches

no postcards

the plane is a rational object

schematics and maths given flight
nothing about god or the spirit
in the wings / riding the wings

my agent, a rational object
the same size as a mannequin

slightly sweating on an overcast day
full of sunday nightmares about

the day he returns to the office
and reads the handover notes

from his temporary replacement
will i still be there? i ask for faith & terrible love

i ask for an open sky

my FBI agent takes me on a date

and decorates her hair with crane flies
prawn cocktail lips / when i said *scare me*
she listened
badly

the words printed out / maybe old dots burning
or ink that starts to disintegrate
when the paper's
handled

which means she read / what i said was fine
and i hate anything with a see-through body
plastic wings dancing
no,

it's the legs are wrong in the air like that
it's the compartments, the exoskeleton
it's that she doesn't know
how

& she pries me open early

& she has teeth that she thinks give more pleasure
at the cracking / she says i will like it

that she has heard fear / makes us braver people in the end

& she eats from within

my FBI agent raises a toast

may we never have friends / as long
as we are able / to forget

the troubles / the hell will
may our house always / follow you
for the rest of your life

if we ever disagree / i wish you luck
may you live / with misfortune

may your house always be
too small / to follow

may your coffin / live all the days
of your life

here's to us / our last survivor
old books to burn / they were too short

may you never disagree
may you never / if your health
falters / raise a glass to us

too short / too small / your house
a glass to your voice / clear and loud

may we never be / as close as
not enough days / friends

to hell with all of
those who

will follow you / your coffin
is there / for the rest of your life

my FBI agent dreams

of flying across antarctica in winter
        the engine starting to give out

i tell her it's going
        to be ok

a big meal waiting for her
        painful air

broken ribs / when she breathes
a dog on her heels

hot sour dog breath, like spray
from breaking ocean / sickness

across the sea / what you share
with me / chasing me down the street

because you found my purse, no
i never lost it / bless

a churning mess
and the tiny spikes for wings

and the albatross, ahead
wings tied together and somehow
beating

Acknowledgements

'poem for my FBI agent, 'my FBI agent is a mathematical problem', and 'my FBI agent talks me through my facebook ad settings' were all first published at Queen Mob's Tea House.

'my FBI agent doesn't like to read' was first published in issue 25 of *The White Review*.

'my FBI agent appears to me in a pub in leytonstone' was first published in issue 19 of *Lighthouse*, from Gatehouse Press.

I want to thank:

Amy Acre for her wonderful work on this book;

all of the writing groups and communities I've been part of over the past decade or so (!), including Roddy Lumsden's Wednesday group, and the Carmelites, who helped me feel like I could write again;

all of my friends for being supportive when I said "I've started writing some poems inspired by a meme that is already kind of dead." I especially want to thank Morgan, Cis, Kat, Kathy, Emma, Lydia, Annie, Richard, Adham, Owen, and Kristin;

my family - thanks forever to Mum, Dad, Ben, Granny, and Max;

and thanks to Tom, who is somehow not sick of any of this yet. I did it!

New and recent titles from Bad Betty Press

bloodthirsty for marriage
Susannah Dickey

The Body You're In
Phoebe Wagner

*And They Are Covered
in Gold Light*
Amy Acre

She Too Is a Sailor
Antonia Jade King

While I Yet Live
Gboyega Odubanjo

No Weakeners
Tim Wells

Blank
Jake Wild Hall

Alter Egos
Edited by Amy Acre
and Jake Wild Hall

Raft
Anne Gill

The Death of a Clown
Tom Bland

Forthcoming in 2020

At the Speed of Dark
Gabriel Akamo

Animal Experiments
Anja Konig

Sylvanian Family
Summer Young

War Dove
Troy Cabida

A Terrible Thing
Gita Ralleigh

Rheuma
William Gee